IF NO ONE WAS THERE FOR YOU...

IF NO ONE WAS THERE FOR YOU...

Overcoming Childhood Trauma
──USING THE──
B. R. E. A. T. H. E. Technique™

DR. JENNIFER THOMAS

DEDICATION

This book is dedicated to the millions of men and
women who have survived childhood trauma.

ACKNOWLEDGMENTS

Thank you God for inspiring my passion to
help childhood trauma survivors live up to their
true calling concerning their lives.

With great respect and admiration, I would like to thank
Donna Partow. This book would not have been possible
without your mentorship and support. You are such
an amazing woman. Your quiet spirit and patience
is to be emulated by all.

CONTENTS

BREATHE

B

Be Honest with yourself about yourself

R

Reclaim your power

E

Experience your emotions

A

Ask for help

T

Tell your story

H

Healthy "Me" time

E

Envision your healing

Created by Dr. Jennifer Thomas

PREFACE

Childhood memories should be some of the most precious memories a child will ever have, but for many of you, your childhood is anything but memorable. Growing up with abuse and neglect was a normal part of your life.

Many of you did not have the type of childhood like a made for television movie. If you are brutally honest, some parts of your childhood were awfully painful, and you would rather not remember them. You have carefully tucked them into the back of your memory. Avoiding your painful childhood memories may cause biological, psychological, behavioral, or sociological problems resulting from unresolved traumatic events.

There has been a concerted effort in recent years to raise awareness about the mental health crisis in the United States. All across this nation, silent tears have gone unseen and silent cries unheard, with millions of children suffering from childhood trauma every year and thousands of adults living with unresolved trauma as a result.

Stars like the late Naomi Judd, Tyler Perry, and Oprah Winfrey have spoken candidly about their struggles with childhood trauma. In addition, many Christians have started to come forward and share their struggles with mental illness and childhood trauma to bring awareness to this mental health crisis.

Despite the many efforts to bring attention to this crisis, many who need help do not seek or get help. Many of you are afraid to seek help because of the stigma attached to mental health treatment. Some of you are afraid to admit you need help for fear of what people will think or say. Some of you may fear being labeled as 'crazy' or losing your jobs because of society's negative views of those with mental illness. For the rest of you, you simply do not recognize that you need help.

Maybe you believe the anger you display is just a part of your DNA or personality. You think you were destined to have anger issues because your parent had anger issues. Have you asked yourself why your parent was always angry? It may come as a surprise, but anger is a common symptom many psychological disorders. Over thirty-two disorders list anger as a symptom.

Your parent's anger may have been due to unresolved childhood trauma or a mental health condition. It is true; anger can *run* in your family through genetics. But, you can also learn angry tendencies from your parents or relatives called *learned behaviors*. The bottom line is that your anger may be from learned behaviors or a mental health disorder and not genetics.

Some of you who have experienced childhood trauma live in isolation. You dismiss the need to isolate yourself as just being an introvert, not knowing that, in actuality, the tendency to avoid social interactions is a characteristic of the effects of childhood trauma. Unless you learn how childhood trauma affects you, you will continue to repeat the same damaging patterns that keep you stuck and hurting.

Research has shown that adversities early in life are a major risk factor for developing psychological and emotional problems in adulthood. Early life adversities have also been linked to higher rates of suicidality, depression, anxiety disorders, post-traumatic stress disorder (PTSD), and aggressive behaviors, to name a few. Childhood trauma is a commonality in adults with substance and alcohol abuse.

In my nearly ten years of working in mental health services, one commonality among the people I worked with is they have experienced childhood trauma. The other commonality is that most have not received mental health treatment for their trauma.

I know it is not easy asking for help, especially when the stigma about mental health treatment makes you feel weak or flawed. You may even shy away from seeking help due to shame and fear about seeking help. There may be one or many reasons you chose not to seek help, but research has shown that mental health issues may become more severe if you ignore them and do not get help.

If you are reading this book, you either know that you have unresolved childhood trauma or something is going on in your life that makes you think you have unresolved trauma. Are you ready to begin your journey to healing from your childhood trauma? Are you ready to become free from your past and truly live? The steps identified in this book can help you begin the journey to your healing and ultimately freedom from your painful past.

INTRODUCTION

Some children have had some of the most amazing childhoods. They have wonderful relationships with their parents and siblings and fond memories of summer vacations at Disneyland, trips to the beach, waking up on Christmas morning waiting for Santa to arrive, dinner at the table as a family, and being hugged and kissed goodnight before going to bed.

Sadly, this is not the case for nearly 35 million children exposed to adverse childhood experiences (ACEs). To put that into perspective, that is almost half of the total number of American children. Many of whom do not receive treatment for their problem.

The number of children who do not receive treatment continues to rise with incidences of trauma and abuse right under our noses. One day while sitting outside under a pavilion attempting to get some work done, a little girl named Addie walked up and sat beside me and started talking and asking me questions. Like many other little children, she was pretty curious.

I try to always take disruption in my plans as a divine moment orchestrated by God. So, instead of acting as if she was disturbing me, I patiently responded to each one of her questions. After asking the typical questions, "What is your name?" and "What are you doing?" She wanted to know more about what I was doing, and I said, "I came out here so that I could write." After a string of questions about what I was writing, I finally asked her if it was something that she wanted to share with me about her.

As she began to talk about herself, I noticed her words were more deliberate. She informed me that she lived with her grandmother. I asked her why she was living with her grandmother. Addie explained that her younger sister lived with her mother. However, she was not allowed to live with her mother because of the abuse between her and her father. She was evasive with the details about the abuse, and because of my mental and behavioral health background, I knew not to pry.

She told me she used to go to counseling, but her grandmother took her out of counseling. Her grandmother felt she no longer needed it. I asked if she informed her grandmother that she felt as if she still needed to go to counseling. She said yes, but she would not listen to her.

Addie sat and talked to me for a long time while the children played on the playground. She shared stories about her friends, friends who were really not her friends, and her goals and ambitions, but Addie never returned to the story about her father and why she lived with her grandmother. She really just needed someone to talk to who would just simply listen.

When Addie left, I felt a sense of sadness because it was clear she was reaching out for help but was not getting it. At that moment, with Addie, I was reminded why I wanted to learn more about the effect of unresolved childhood trauma on adults and how to overcome it. The sad reality is there are more children just like her.

Like Addie, some of you are not getting the mental health treatment you need. According to Mental Health America (MHA) statistics, over half of United States (U.S.) adults who have a mental illness are not receiving treatment. This means that over twenty-seven million adults are going untreated. Adults and youth alike lack adequate insurance coverage. This means that even if there is a need for mental health care, some parents or caregivers will not be able to afford to pay for treatment. Can you imagine a child asking for help and being told by a trusted adult that they do not need help? Can you imagine a child seeking help, but no one listens or seems to care.

People are not getting the help they desperately need because society's beliefs about mental illness cause people with mental health problems to be treated differently from those with physical illnesses. The treatment of the problem and the treatment of the person look different. If you have mental health issues, it is rarely taken as seriously as physical health issues.

This disparity can range from negative societal perceptions to discrimination in health coverage. It is validated when the parents or caregivers have ambivalent feelings about a child asking for mental health help, such as in the case of Addie. This faulty thinking is based on the fact that it is easier for someone to see when you are physically sick than mentally ill. After all, from the outside, you can look completely "normal."

A mental illness is often "invisible" because, unlike a broken bone that can be seen, the pain of a "broken brain" cannot be seen by the naked eye. The sad reality is that in the minds of the onlookers, the illness or its effects must be seen for it to be real. In addition, mental health treatment is seen as an option, whereas treatment relating to physical health is considered necessary. If you had a cancer diagnosis, you would rarely be told not to get treatment. Having a mental illness is just as real as being physically ill; the difference is a person with a physical illness receives the proper treatment, is cared for, and has someone to talk to about their illness. Above all, society treats those with physical illnesses with the respect, seriousness, and legitimacy it deserves.

People with mental illness are marginalized and discriminated against. Michelle Obama said it best when she said, "At the root of this dilemma is the way mental health in this country. Whether an illness affects your heart, your leg, or your brain, it is still an illness, and there should be no distinction." Children who do not get help will grow to become adults with unresolved trauma. What happens with the unresolved trauma depends on the person.

CHAPTER 1

WHAT IS CHILDHOOD TRAUMA?

What exactly is childhood trauma? Childhood trauma is just as the word suggests. It is any traumatic events that happened to you before you became an adult or until age eighteen. Childhood trauma is a term used to describe any significant experience that overwhelms your ability to function and cope. Trauma comes from the Greek word that means 'wound.' The Greek word wound describes a physical wound. Today when we speak of trauma, we are referring to psychological wounds.

You may have heard the following saying, "What goes on in this house stays in this house." It is a proverbial statement that created an unwritten rule in many homes across this country and has wreaked havoc on many of your lives. The saying opened the door and let the predators and abusers in your homes. It means that only the people residing in the house are privy to what is happening inside it. In other words, do not let outsiders into family business. Because of this saying, many of you have endured harm, mistreatment, or even abuse at the hands of someone close to you.

Another one of those proverbial sayings is, "It's our secret." This saying has kept you bound to your trauma by swearing you to secret. You continue to keep the pain of the trauma because someone manipulated you into silence. Sadly, many are still enduring the same harm, mistreatment, and abuse as an adult because you fear telling the truth for fear of failing the person who abused you. You are more concerned with keeping their secret than getting your healing.

As in the case of "It is our secret," The secret was unspoken, but it is always between you. This means that although you have not talked about it, it is still a problem that separates you and the person. Keeping secrets is a burden. It is a burden that you do not have to bear.

You may fear being judged because of what happened to you. Once you reveal the secret, you will be set free from being consumed with worry about others finding out the truth.

It appears to be the belief that as a person ages, they miraculously forget the pains of their past. Trauma is not amnesic. If I had a dollar for every time that I have heard someone say, "They should be over that by now." or "That happened a long time ago.," I would be rich. There is not a set time to recover from a traumatic event. People who have told you that "The past is the past.," "How long will you play the victim?" or "Just get over it." do not understand trauma and its lasting psychological effect that can remain with you for a lifetime or until you heal from the trauma.

While some trauma experiences are easy to overcome, others experiences can trouble you for years. Contrary to belief, it is not easy to *get over* childhood trauma. The timeline for healing varies from person to person, and even what recovery looks like varies from person to person. It is impossible to predict how long you will experience the effects of the trauma. What is important for you to know is that recovering from trauma is a process that may take a long time. It is no surprise that people 50, 60, or even 70 years old still have lingering effects from the trauma that they experienced in their childhood.

Recovery does not necessarily mean complete freedom from the traumatic event, nor does it mean that you can no longer recall events relating to the trauma. In general, recovery is the ability to live in the present moment while thoughts of your past are not so debilitating that you cannot move forward.

The physical scars of your traumatic childhood event may not always be seen, but if left untreated and unresolved, the psychological and emotional scars will be seen long after the event. Regardless of how long your past trauma occurred or its extent, you can still overcome it and go on to live a successful and fulfilling life.

Studies have shown that if you have experienced childhood trauma, you will often demonstrate core deficits in the capacity to regulate physiological and emotional responses. You may have difficulty understanding what you feel, where it comes from, how to cope with it, or how to express what you are feeling.

How you make meaning of your life is built upon and strongly influenced by your beliefs about your experience. Your beliefs, whether negative or positive, influence your interpretations, emotional responses, and action. The first years of your life are the building blocks that predicate the trajectory of your life and are important for building a foundation for your future.

These years are your formative years. They are especially crucial for your physical, intellectual, and emotional development. Your mental wellness may be impacted if you do not grow up in a safe and secure environment. If you have experienced childhood trauma, it may lead to setbacks as an adult because there is a possibility that you will emerge from a traumatic childhood so damaged by those abusive years that you may never live up to your full potential.

When you have been traumatized as a child, it is a soul wound that lives deep inside you. David said in the book of Psalm, "For my soul is full of troubles: and my life draweth nigh unto the grave. I am counted with them that go down into the pit: I am as a man that hath no strength." (Psalm 88:3-4 KJV). A soul wound is an event that is so painful that it pierces the very core of your existence. Your soul consists of three parts: mind, will, and emotions. It is the part of you that drives you to be who God has called you to be on earth.

Traumatic experiences can impact all aspects of your mind, body, and spirit, whether based on a real or perceived threat. Some people associate trauma with being involved in a violent life-threatening event. In reality, trauma involves circumstances you *perceive* as highly threatening to you physically, emotionally, or both. An event does not have to involve physical harm to be traumatic.

A traumatic event is any event that causes physical, emotional, spiritual, or psychological harm. The event can be shocking, frightening, scary, or dangerous. It is not the actual events of the experience that determines whether the event is traumatic but rather your emotional and cognitive impact of the experience. In other words, the more frightened and helpless you feel, the more likely you will be traumatized.

Trauma comes in many forms and looks different from one person to the next. Trauma is subjective. It means a traumatic event is not an event perceived equally by those who experience it. What is traumatic to you may not necessarily impact someone else who has experienced the same traumatic event.

The fact is that the same event or experience will affect people differently. No one can say that just because you experienced the same traumatic event and were not traumatized, another person will not be traumatized because of it. A parent's divorce that stays with one person for decades may be brushed off after a short time by someone else.

Similarly, what adults perceive as traumatic may differ from what a child perceives as traumatic. A child may experience trauma after a major car accident, whereas the adult in the car is not affected. A traumatic event can be an event that happens one time or exposure to a repeated, prolonged, harmful, or stressful event. The trauma does not have to be something that happens directly to the child. A child can experience trauma by witnessing the traumatic event happening to someone else.

A friend of mine, Jane, grew up in a home with domestic violence. She shared her story about what it was like living in her home and witnessing her father trying to kill her mother. Jane said she never remembered her father showing love and affection. She remembers that her family did not have a lot, but when her father was not at home, they had "peace and quiet." Her mother would sleep with an iron pipe for protection.

Jane told of a time when her father came home and entered the room where she and her mother were sleeping. He turned the light on and snatched the covers off of her mother. He began cutting her with a switchblade knife on the side of the arm where little 4-year-old Jane was lying. Her mother pulled the pole from where she had it stored and began hitting her father to get him off her. Jane and her mother survived the incident, but Jane was left severely traumatized.

Jane is still traumatized by this event that happened over 60 years ago. Jane is an example of a person who did not receive mental health treatment but could have benefited from the treatment. Also, at that time, mental health treatment was virtually unheard of in black communities across the U.S. Jane still has trauma triggers relating to the event.

When you experience a traumatic event, your brain often stores the memory based on what you are feeling and sensing at the time of the trauma. When your brain recognizes the same trauma in your present situation as your past trauma, it activates the fight, flight, freeze, flop, or friend response, even if you are not in danger. This is called a trauma trigger response.

The triggers are what activates your subconscious and bring back strong memories. It can cause you to feel like you are living through it all over again. Triggers can include sights, sounds, smells, or thoughts that remind you of the traumatic event in some way. It may be certain smells, a particular song or sound, or even the weather.

Trauma triggers are unique to the individual. Anything that reminds you of what happened before or during trauma is a potential trigger. All triggers are not bad. I was walking recently, and the weather reminded me of a happy time at my first military duty station over thirty years ago.

For people who have experienced trauma, triggers can be terrifying. Jane's triggers are when she hears loud noises or people talking too loud. She suddenly becomes afraid. She still does not like to play any games where she may be held or pinned down (i.e., wrestling and horse playing). The responses to trauma are individualized. Trauma triggers vary between people and can be a variety of events and are unpredictable.

Trauma looks different in each person, and it is sometimes hard to understand the different types of trauma. Trauma comes in several categories, such as acute, chronic, vicarious, or mass trauma; technically, no trauma is worse than the other in terms of its effect on your mental health. There is no way of telling how trauma will affect you. Someone may say, "It was not that bad." Easily dismissed events could have been traumatic for you, even if someone else thinks it was not that bad. No one can tell you how an event affects you but you or if the event is "bad enough" to be traumatizing.

Research has revealed that childhood trauma is common among all races and socioeconomic backgrounds. However, childhood trauma often is not identified, acknowledged, or addressed in the minority populations (i.e., Latinos and African Americans) due to several factors, including the lack of affordable mental health care, the cultural stigma surrounding care, discrimination, and lack of awareness among the minority population about mental health.

Research has also found that Adverse Childhood Experiences (ACEs) can profoundly impact an adult's health outcomes later in life. ACEs are events or situations that can negatively impact a child's mental and physical development. While ACEs carry the potential to cause trauma symptoms, it is essential to note that not all children who experience ACEs have trauma. To better explain, you can look at ACEs and their relationship to trauma like a car accident. A car *collides* with your vehicle. The *collision* leaves a *dent* in your vehicle. The *collision* is the ACE, and the resulting *dent* is the trauma. A car *collides* with your vehicle, and there is *no subsequent dent*. In this case, the ACE did not result in trauma.

However, research has shown a significant relationship between ACEs and trauma. ACEs are anything that can disrupt a child's sense of safety. The following is a list of possible ACEs:

- Child physical abuse
- Child sexual abuse
- Child emotional abuse
- Emotional neglect
- Physical neglect
- Mentally ill or suicidal person in the home
- Growing up in a household with substance abuse
- Witnessing domestic violence in the home
- Loss of a parent to death or abandonment
- Parental divorce
- Incarceration of a family member of the household
- Verbal humiliation
- Bullying
- Natural Disasters
- Vehicle accidents or other accidents

If you are suffering from childhood trauma, you most likely endured an ACE from the list. Unfortunately, ACEs are not rare. Statistics point to a significant portion of the population struggling with the adverse effects of trauma.

In addition, research on ACEs identifies a link to chronic health problems, mental illness, substance misuse, and adult incarceration. Studies also indicate that childhood trauma is high among incarcerated individuals. Childhood trauma has also been linked to a shorter life expectancy. ACEs increase risky health behaviors like smoking and having a large number of sexual partners. Also, studies have shown that individuals who are sexually abused as a child are three times more likely to have ideation and attempts, according to a new study in Psychological Medicine.

If you are looking for a mental health diagnosis for childhood trauma, you will not find it. Childhood trauma is not a specific diagnosis listed in the American Psychiatric Association's Diagnostic and Statistical Manual of Mental Disorders, 5th Edition (DSM-5), the manual that licensed mental health practitioners use to diagnose a mental health condition. Although not listed in the DSM as a stand-alone diagnosis, trauma is a risk factor for nearly all behavioral health and substance use disorders.

Each year, thousands of children experience some form of childhood abuse. According to a National Survey of Children's Health (NSCH) survey, approximately thirty-five million children in the United States have experienced at least one type of childhood trauma. The Center for Disease Control (CDC) estimates that approximately 61 percent of adults experience childhood trauma before they are 18 years old.

Suppose you have suffered loss, abuse, or neglect early in your life; it may lead to severe psychological, physiological, and emotional disorders for years after the traumatic event. Childhood trauma symptoms may appear in adulthood in the form of developmental or mental health disorders. The damaging and traumatic effects of experiencing childhood trauma can last a lifetime.

As you grow, your understanding of the world grows and changes; it is strongly influenced by your experiences, whether good or bad. Your experiences dictate the choices you make and determine the direction that your life takes. All your assumptions are formed by your past experiences and begin with what you believe of yourself and others.

You may even have problems forming healthy relationships because children do not know how to process a traumatic event, especially if a loved one committed the offense. Whether the trauma that happened to you was physical, sexual, or emotional, the impact can show up in your relationships.

The first relationship harmed after a trauma is the relationship with yourself. The trauma that you experience disconnected you from a healthy sense of self. You may have begun to believe the lies, such as "No one will ever want you," "You're ugly," "You're stupid," "You're dumb," "You're fat," "You will never amount to anything," that were said to you by those who you trusted and were supposed to love you and provide a safe and happy environment.

You may now believe you can no longer trust anyone because of what happened to you. You may have told yourself that if I stay closed off, unsociable, or guarded, I will not allow anyone to hurt me again. Have you heard the proverbial statement, "I do not need anyone but myself?" These are the words spoken by a deeply hurt person who no longer has faith or trust in anyone—a person whose trust system is destroyed.

The trauma you experienced convinced you that you cannot depend on others because the chances are you will get hurt again. You instinctively push everyone away. If you decide to trust, it will be on your own terms. It causes you to have control issues. You want to control everyone and everything around you. If you are not in control, you walk away from the relationship.

A long history of being victimized or traumatized by people you trust makes trusting very difficult. However, reaching a place where you can let go is the only way to resolve the trauma fully. Just remember that by letting go, you do not forget what happened to you but rather recognize, understand and forgive the faults of others.

Many of you have told yourselves that you are flawed, not good enough, and unworthy of anyone's love because of what happened to you. Thoughts like these can wreak havoc in every one of your relationships. You may not be able to show or reciprocate love because you do not know what love is. If someone wants to form a friendship with you, you immediately become suspicious of their intentions.

Experiencing childhood trauma can also impact the way that you form romantic relationships. The psychology of attachment styles looks at how you form close, long-term bonds that are formed first with your caregivers and then with others throughout your lifespan. Let us look at the types of attachment styles in relationships. There are four adult attachment styles: Anxious (Preoccupied), Avoidant (Dismissive), Disorganized (Fearful-Avoidant), and Secure. The following information may help identify your relationship style.

Anxious/Preoccupied

- Negative self-image
- A positive view of others
- Seeks approval
- Strong fear of abandonment
- Preoccupied with the relationship

- Desperate for love
- Prone to pushing others away
- Over-analyze information
- Overthink (even your own words and actions)
- Clingy
- Overly jealous

Avoidant/Dismissive

- Perception of being a "lone wolf"
- Strong
- Independent
- Self-sufficient
- High self-esteem
- Avoids conflict by denying own needs
- Fears rejection
- People depend on you
- Avoids emotional closeness
- Hide/suppress feelings
- Described by others as detached and prefers solitude
- Annoyed by others who express desires or feelings
- Highly successful and competent
- Difficulty trusting and letting others in

Disorganized/Fearful-Avoidant

- Unstable and ambiguous behaviors
- Indecisive about seeking a lot of reassurance and withdrawing
- Do not want intimacy and closeness

- Trouble trusting and depending on others
- Avoid strong emotional attachment for fear of getting hurt

Secure

- Relationships based on honesty, tolerance, and emotional closeness
- Do not fear being alone
- Do not depend on responsiveness and approval from partner
- Positive view of themselves and others
- Attuned to their emotions
- Comfortable with intimacy

You may be wondering why is understanding my attachment style important? Attachment styles are some common behaviors seen in relationships. When faced with difficult situations, you may default to learned behaviors that are not necessarily appropriate. Knowing your attachment style helps you to recognize insecure attachment styles that may be part of the reason for your failing relationships.

John Bowlby developed the attachment theory and believed the emotional bond that did not form between the child and the primary caregivers has a lifelong negative impact. Your attachment style is formed by your personal experiences in your childhood and the type of relationship you had with your parents or primary caregivers.

Identifying your attachment style will help you recognize unhealthy relationship behaviors and understand why you continue to repeat the same pattern of behaviors in all of your relationships. You may not see a characteristic that fits you on the list because it is not all-inclusive. It is also possible to have more than one attachment style.

Let us take a look at your possible attachment style. I say 'possible' because someone can grow up in the ideal environment and be the opposite of their attachment style based on the list of behaviors consistent with a particular attachment style.

For example, if you grew up in a home where you did not feel loved, you might be anxious (preoccupied). If you grew up in a home where the primary caregivers were not available or dismissive, or as a child you had to take care of yourself, you are most likely the avoidant (dismissive) type. If you grew up in a home with abuse or neglect and you remember feeling afraid and distrustful of your parents. You may be the disorganized (fearful-avoidant) type. Lastly, if you experienced positive relationships and love throughout your childhood, you will most of the time be securely attached.

In addition to relationship problems relating to childhood trauma, there is also a risk for health problems. Research has also shown that exposure to traumatic events during childhood can dramatically increase your risk for serious health problems, including heart disease, stroke, and cancer. Studies have shown that if you have unresolved trauma, you may also be prone to mental health problems such as anxiety and depression. You may also be at a greater risk for various physical ailments.

It is said that you are the sum total of your experiences. Those experiences, whether positive or negative, make you the person you are today. Those experiences also influence positively or negatively each decision that you make concerning your life and your future. In other words, your childhood experiences shape your future. How you think, grow, feel, and act as children can be compared to the foundation of a building. An architect will tell you that the rule of thumb for a building is that the taller the building is, the stronger the foundation needs to be.

You can use this analogy as it relates to life. The farther you want to go in life, the stronger the "foundation" of your childhood needs to be. So, does it means a building will not stand erect because of an unstable foundation? Not necessarily. Even so, just because you have experienced childhood trauma does not mean you will not thrive because you grew up in an unstable environment. Some of the most successful people in the world have experienced some form of childhood trauma. I mentioned some earlier in the book.

The Leaning Tower of Pisa is leaning because of its unstable foundation, yet the building is still standing. Today, the tower is one of Europe's most beautiful architectural structures. Who would have guessed that what started as a design flaw is now an integral part of what draws more than five million visitors each year to the tower? You can also take events from your traumatic past and use them to make a better future, a future complete with resolved pain, good health, and healthy relationships. You may have a greater appreciation and a renewed sense of purpose and meaning in your life by having experienced trauma. I am in no way downplaying the painful effects of the trauma. I want you to know that healing is possible, and you can turn your tragedy into triumph.

A study was conducted with four hundred successful people. When researchers looked at their lives, they found that seventy-five percent of the research participants had experienced childhood trauma, yet they were highly successful. The bible tells us in Romans 8:28, "And we know that all things work together for good to them that love God, to them who are the called according to his purpose."

You can see a powerful example of the Lord's omniscient plan of all things working for your good in the biblical account of the story of Esther. The story of Esther is an amazing story that depicts how God used one woman to impact the lives of the Jewish people.

Besides being a woman in Susa, where women were treated subservient to men, Esther was also poor and an orphan. It appeared that all odds were against her, yet, God had great plans for her life, just like He has great plans for your life. This is only one story of overcoming adversity in the bible. There are others. You, too, can take the broken pieces of your past and make your life a masterpiece.

Children are seen as highly resilient and able to bounce back or pull through from just about any adversity. Generally speaking, resilience is the capacity to adapt to challenges positively. The substantial number of adults suffering from childhood trauma proves that children are not as resilient as once thought.

In my career working with adults with mental health issues, childhood trauma has significantly impacted their adult lives. It is my belief that what we, as adults, see as resilience is internalized pain in some children. Children have learned to hide and internalize their pain through fear of harm rather than resolve it. Those who internalize their pain will focus harm on themselves rather than attacking someone else. If a child does not have an opportunity to deal effectively with their emotions relating to the trauma, they will internalize it, and it will manifest in different ways, such as anger, self-blame or self-hatred.

When you hear someone say that people, more specifically children are resilient, you may automatically think that this means that traumatic events that happened to you as a child should not still bother you as an adult. This is not the case. Children are resilient but not made out of steel. They have feelings, and if they are not acknowledged, we, society, will sooner or later see and experience the result of that child not receiving the REAL HELP they needed.

A number of adults reported having experienced ACEs in their childhood. Research conducted by the CDC found that more than 60 percent of American adults experienced at least one ACE, and almost a quarter of adults have experienced three or more ACEs in their childhood.

In addition, childhood trauma leaves a lasting impact on your emotional health as a child that, if left unresolved, will affect your emotional health as an adult. It will continue to affect you until you identify, process, and resolve what happened to you. You may have been taught as a child to tuck your feelings away. As a result, you learn to hide your feelings, and over time, this can impact your mental health, especially when experiencing trauma. Unspoken traumatic experiences in childhood can have severe and long-lasting effects well into adulthood if left unresolved.

Childhood trauma is linked to substance use (i.e., alcohol, drugs, smoking, mental health disorders, and health conditions). There are many adverse long-term effects of childhood trauma. For some, the consequences of childhood trauma are more severe than others. The more extreme the trauma, the higher your risk of experiencing long-term difficulties. Research has also shown that you will have a greater chance of developing health and psychological conditions after experiencing a traumatic childhood event, including:

- Anxiety
- Cancer
- Depression
- Diabetes
- Heart problems
- Eating disorders
- Anger
- Addictive behaviors
- Post-traumatic stress disorder (PTSD)
- Stroke
- Substance use disorders
- Suicidal ideation

Post-traumatic stress disorder (PTSD) from Childhood Trauma

One of the most common diagnoses associated with childhood trauma is Post-traumatic Stress Disorder (PTSD). In the previous versions of the DSM-5, PTSD was included under anxiety disorders. However, PTSD is now included in the category of Trauma and Stressor Related Disorder (TSRD).

The conditions included in this classification require exposure to a traumatic or stressful event as a diagnostic criterion. Exposure to a traumatic event during your childhood is the risk for PTSD. According to the American Psychiatric Association (APA), PTSD is a psychiatric disorder involving extreme distress and disruption of daily living due to exposure to a traumatic event. The DSM-5 divides PTSD symptoms into four categories:

1. Intrusive Symptoms
2. Avoidance
3. Negative changes in thoughts and mood
4. Changes in arousal and reactivity

If you have a history of childhood trauma, you may experience problems in the following areas:

- Hypervigilance
- Addiction to gambling or shopping
- Feelings of alienation
- Feelings of hopelessness
- Low self-esteem
- Difficulty forming relationships/attachment issues
- Unhealthy relationships

Suicide and Suicidal Ideation

Suicide and suicidal ideation deserve additional attention. According to the Center for Disease Control (CDC), over 45,000 people die from suicide every year. Research has shown consistent support for a strong link between childhood trauma and suicide completion.

Childhood trauma has been associated with an increased risk for suicide attempts and suicidal ideation in adults. I recently conducted research on the "Correlation between Adverse Childhood Experiences and its relationship to suicidality among Air Force Airmen." My research identified a direct correlation between childhood trauma and suicidal ideation among military members. These findings are not only significant for our military members but are also significant for others who have experienced childhood trauma.

The findings suggest that understanding the effects of childhood trauma is important in the clinical assessment and treatment of suicidal ideation for adults who have been harmed as a child. Research has confirmed that unresolved childhood trauma is a risk factor in suicidal ideation, and the ideation increases with age and can possibly lead to death by suicide.

Approximately two-thirds of suicides among adults are linked to childhood trauma. My research confirmed that childhood sexual abuse strongly predicts suicidal ideation. There are higher suicide rates among those who have experienced prolonged childhood trauma.

There is compelling research that military members who have experienced childhood trauma are at a greater risk for suicide. In particular, research by Kathleen Lapp concluded that ninety-six percent of male veterans experienced some form of victimization during their lifetime. In addition, suicide among army soldiers has been linked to childhood trauma. The safety and security of our military should be of the utmost importance beginning with understanding the barriers to mental health care among military members. In addition, research has shown that of the individuals who attempted suicide, approximately eighty percent had experienced at least one type of ACE.

Response to Trauma

When you experience a traumatic event, your body reacts in several ways. One way is through disturbed sleep. Chronic stress increases cortisol, often referred to as stress hormone, which disrupts sleep cycles that can lead to sleep disorders.

Research has shown a causal relationship between sleep and emotional brain functions. This is the part of your brain responsible for emotions, feelings, and instincts. Sustained cortisol increases can harm the brain and impair thinking, memory, and learning.

It is not unusual to have difficulty thinking and processing, called "going blank," when cortisol interferes with brain activity. Sleep is closely connected to mental and emotional health. Sleep abnormalities are also identified in nearly all mood and anxiety disorders.

Do you know that you can manifest physical pain in your body through unresolved painful thoughts and emotions? Research has identified some connections between emotional issues and physical diseases. For example, Dr. Ryke Hamer's research has shown a correlation between patients with unresolved trauma and cancer.

He believes that every health issue is rooted in an emotional issue. Dr. Hamer began looking at the relationship between emotional health and disease after his youngest son died from a gunshot wound in an accidental shooting. A few months after the tragic death of his son, Dr. Hamer found he had testicular cancer.

His wife also had developed cancer. He began to wonder if this diagnosis might be related to the tragic loss of his son. As a result, he began researching the personal history of cancer patients to determine whether they had experienced a significant traumatic event before their cancer diagnosis.

After looking at over 20,000 cases, he found a relationship between experiencing severe psychological and emotional trauma and a cancer diagnosis. Not only did he find the relationship between trauma and cancer, but he also discovered that every cancer had a different emotional cause. For example, cancer in the left breast was caused by an emotional conflict involving a child, home, or mother. It is common for those with cancer to have suppressed emotions, particularly anger, over an extended time.

Dr. Hamer found from his research that most of his patients experienced a traumatic event, usually two years before their diagnosis. Although Dr. Hamer's findings are contrary to western medicine teachings and conventional treatment measures, it presents a new way of looking at your emotions affect your physical health.

In addition, loneliness has been determined to be a risk factor for disease. If a person has been deprived of affection and acceptance early in life, they develop a sensitivity to the needs of others while suppressing their own emotional needs. These are the people that is often referred to as caretakers. Caretakers get their validation from helping others while refusing to accept help for themselves from others. It may have come from being taught not to be selfish as a child. Seeing accepting help as selfish results in a lifetime of emotional suppression. When you go through a traumatic event, you may feel like you cannot tell anyone; therefore, you needlessly suffer in silence.

Emotional suppression may serve as an essential purpose and necessary step in the healing process. If you experience a traumatic event, you may initially suppress your emotions to evaluate the situation to respond to it better. However, suppressed emotions do not go away. They are buried in your subconscious.

Your subconscious is a powerful force and repository for all of your past traumas, feelings, thoughts (good and bad), and experiences. The subconscious is different from the conscious mind. The unconscious mind is defined as the deepest level of your mind. It is the part of the mind that regulates your involuntary functions.

The subconscious never sleeps. It remembers things that you do not remember. The subconscious mind can be described as a sponge that soaks up memories of your past thoughts, actions, and the spoken words of those around you. If a mother calls a child 'fat' even jokingly, the subconscious mind remembers those words and stores them. A recent study by UCLA psychologists found that children who are called fat at a young age are more likely to be obese in adulthood. How you develop false beliefs in early childhood impacts you for the rest of your lives.

When you receive information from spoken words, it is stored in your subconscious. What happens with that information depends on whether you accept or reject the information. It is the basis for your perception of self and explains why childhood experiences determine the direction of our lives. It explains why children can grow up in the same household with the same parents and experience the same trauma, yet the traumatic event does not affect them the same.

One may receive the negative information while the other child rejects the information. It is also important to remember that your written or spoken words are stored in our subconscious that your mind processes as images. Your minds process these written images as spoken words. Your minds hear images as if they are spoken words. It suggests that hearing and vision are intertwined, at least as far as the mind is concerned.

You may have reacted to the trauma by ignoring it. While ignoring your feelings may not affect you in the short term, there may be severe health consequences to bottling your emotions over the long term. Also, suppressed emotions that are bottled up intensify over time and express themselves in other ways, such as anger and aggression. They will keep showing up in your life, in some form of dysfunction or unhappiness, until you resolve them. When you have experienced trauma, you will use defensive tactics to protect yourself from additional trauma.

Your brain has the amygdala and the hippocampus to help you make choices to keep you safe. The amygdala (pronounced uh-MIG-duh-luh) is a structure deep in the brain that is part of the limbic system, often thought of as the "emotional brain."

The amygdala is best known for its fight or flight response. The amygdala's job is to process and express emotions, especially anger and fear, quickly. It is your body's emergency response system. The amygdala activates the fight or flight responses in your body. The amygdala is activated by traumatic stress. It answers the question, "Is this particular event a threat to me?" It provides automatic, rapid, and unconscious reactions to thoughts or events.

The hippocampus' job makes it possible for you to recall memories from the past. Your body will naturally employ emotional trauma responses to keep you safe. When facing trauma, some leave their bodies (dissociate). Others shut off all feelings and go numb. Some build an immediate defense – fight, flight, freeze, flop or flee. You will read real-life examples of a traumatic experience and identify the type of trauma response later in this chapter.

The Five Fs are natural ways your body is automatically programmed to keep you safe: Fight, Flight, Freeze, Flop, and Friend. How you react to trauma varies for each person. It depends on the type and severity of the traumatic event, whether other current stressors exist in your life, available family or community support, your personality, your natural levels of resilience, and if there were any previous traumatic experiences.

There are some common psychological negative reactions to a traumatic event. Below is a graph to define the response and give some examples of common responses to trauma:

	Response Type	Definition	Common Psychological Responses
The Five Fs Chart	FIGHT *Active Defense*	Self -preservation mode. Resist or retaliate without regard to the outcome.	Angry, overt/subtle aggression, automatically see people as an adversary, always feels the need to defend self, explosive outbursts, inward anger, lash out at slight provocation, aggressive language, controlling behaviors, narcissistic tendencies
	FLIGHT *Active Defense*	Running away to escape the danger by seeking to put distance between threat and self.	Avoids confrontation, intentional/unintentional distracted, overachiever, workaholic, thrill-seeker, compulsive behaviors, workaholic, over-worrying, chronically busy, perfectionist, obsessive thinking, unable to relax, a need to stay busy, workaholic tendencies, Perfectionism
	Freeze *Active Defense*	This occurs when our brain sees the threat but determines that fight or flight is not possible. *almost always used by those sexually assaulted	Stay in bed excessively, inability to voice thoughts, inability to communicate feelings, gives up quickly, avoids serious relationships, reclusive, daydreamer, mistrustful of others, lives in solitude, dissociation, isolation, difficulty making decisions, difficulty acting on decisions, feels defeated, perceived as lazy, fear of achieving or trying new things

	Friend *Passive Defense*	Complex response that entails pleasing to reduce harm to ourselves.	People pleasing, inability to say no, over helping, often mistaken for a personality trait, not trauma, accommodating, co-dependent relationships, giving up self for others, low self-esteem, concerned with fitting in, "Yes" person, unable to express true feelings, avoids conflicts
	Flop *Passive Defense*	Our bodies completely stop reacting to the traumatic event. This can lead to the body going limp or into an unconscious state.	Appearing disengaged, lack of emotions, mind/body shut down and becomes compliant to preserve life

When you go through traumatic events, you hold onto the emotions, until the traumatic event is resolved. If you have a range of unresolved childhood traumas living within you, it can possibly make your adult life difficult. Let us now look at the lives of two individuals and how experiencing a traumatic event in their childhood affected them.

As told by Mary

One night I had a conversation with Mary, a seventy-year-old lady with significant health problems. Mary was born into a loving family. Mary is a people pleaser who gives up herself for others. Mary is a darker complexion African American lady. This is important because some African American parents or relatives treat children differently based on the complexion of their skin. This is a term that is referred to as colorism.

Colorism is a form of discrimination where those with lighter skin are treated as more superior and favorably than those with darker skin. It implies that you are less attactive if you have darker skin and beautiful if you have lighter skin. Research has shown that colorism is a source of trauma for minorities, in particular African Americans.

Colorism does not just exist in the African American communities, but it also exists in communities where there are different varieties of skin shades, such as Latin America, the Caribbean, and Southeast Asia. Colorism leads to negative effects on the individual's beliefs about themselves, as well as on their health and interpersonal relationships.

Imagine growing up in a household where your parents held this belief. Children who grow up in this kind of environment where being taught that their dark skin is bad may grow up to foster feelings of self-hatred.

In the conversation with Mary, she spoke about the trauma she experienced as a child due to colorism. She spoke of the pain that she still lives with today because she was mistreated as a child those seventy years ago. She grew up in a household where children were treated differently because of their skin complexion.

She spoke about how the parents treated fair complexion children better than the darker complexion children. As she told her story, I wondered how well she recalled the specifics of the trauma even so many years. She spoke about her childhood events as if she was talking about something that had recently happened.

As years passed, You may expect that the memory of the trauma would dissipate, but in her case, it had not, as with many of you.

This is called enhanced memories. The events are so traumatizing that they are etched in your memories. A number of studies have found that color discrimination in childhood has lead to mental health disorders such as body dysmorphic disorder, body image issues and self-esteem issues in adulthood. Colorism kills the confidence and self-esteem in children and continues into adulthood. Sales of skin-lightening products are predicted to reach over sixteen billion by 2030. The growing preference for fair skin to enhance beauty and confidence is driving the global beauty market growth.

As told by Jackie

Jackie is a fifty-year-old female who had a traumatic childhood based on a failed relationship with her mother. She is easily irritated and quick to anger. Her mother was overbearing and controlling. Jackie's mother allowed her stepfather to abuse her physically. He did not care for Jackie because she was not his biological child. Since the stepfather did not like Jackie, her mother sent her to live with her aunt when she was about seventeen years old.

Jackie lived with her aunt until, according to Jackie, her aunt tried to "pimp her out." She eventually left her aunt's house. She eventually returned to her mother's house. Her mother had a child with her stepfather, whom she treated much better than Jackie. Jackie interpreted this as her mother not loving her.

Although Jackie is successful in her career, from the outside looking in, you can still see a little girl seeking love and affection from her mother. She isolates herself and does not trust easily. She also has health problems and most recently was hospitalized for a serious medical condition.

Jackie has somewhat reconciled with her mother but still does not have an adult-child and mother relationship. Her mother still treats her like a child, presumably because she missed that part of her life by sending her away to live with her sister. In her mother's eyes, she is still that 14-year-old little girl she sent away as a child. Jackie is resentful of the way that her mother treats her. It has caused a rift in their relationship.

Based on these two scenarios, there are two types of trauma responses. You may refer to "The Five Fs chart" to find a description of each response. Mary has a *friend's* response to trauma. Based on the *friend* response to trauma, some characteristics include being a people pleaser, inability to say no, and they give up themselves for others. Jackie has a *fight* response to trauma. Based on the description of the *fight* response, people in the *fight* response feel irritable and are quick to anger. They lash out at people around them over seemingly small things.

Everyone responds to trauma in different ways. Having an understanding of each of the types of trauma response will help you understand your specific behaviors. It can also help you understand why you respond to a negative situation as you do and help you change those negative responses to more positive ones. If you are negatively responding to trauma, you can learn how to respond to stress in healthier ways that can help you improve your life by appropriately responding to negative situations.

Steps to healing from the traumatic experience

Whether you have suffered from anxiety or another mental health disorder and have visited a therapist, you have probably been encouraged to try the breathing technique to manage your mental health concerns. Even if you have not had a mental health concern, someone may have told you to 'just breathe' or 'take a breath' when you appeared distressed. This technique may work for some, but for others, it makes the situation more stressful, especially if you are not able to control your breathing after being told to do so.

Now, in addition to the present stressor, you are faced with an additional stressor of the inability to calm yourself down. What is the purpose of telling someone to 'breathe' or 'take a breath'? The main reason is that drawing attention to your breathing makes you aware of your strained breathing to give you a moment to calm down. In other words, it acts as a distraction to your current situation while bringing you to the present moment.

The BREATHE that you will learn about today is more than the act of taking air into and releasing it from your lungs. It is a seven-step technique to help you walk through your brokenness to wholeness. BREATHE is an acronym I created to help those who have gone through a traumatic event take the necessary steps toward healing.

The process incorporates the basic breathing technique with seven practical steps (BREATHE) to use while you navigate your healing process. These steps were created to walk you through overcoming childhood trauma, but you can also use them with other mental health issues. Whether you have been abused by a close family member, witnessed a traumatic event, or any other traumatic event, you can come out of it using the steps identified in the BREATHE technique™.

Yes, it will be mentally challenging to revisit those memories but BREATHE and take a step forward into your healing. The next chapters will describe the seven steps.

CHAPTER 2

BE HONEST WITH YOURSELF ABOUT YOURSELF

One of the main components of overcoming the effects of childhood trauma is to be honest with yourself about yourself. What do I mean about this? Do you spend a lot of time trying to hide events concerning your childhood or trying to act a certain way to people? You may be presenting a narrative of your life that's inauthentic. This is the time to be free from the pains and hurts of your past. As the Bible states in John 8:32, "the truth shall make you free."

You may not have been allowed to deal with your feelings related to the trauma properly. You were either told to ignore your feelings as if nothing happened to you, and made to feel ashamed because of what happened to you. Some of you were even blamed for the trauma, and because of this, you are not honest about how you are feeling. You may become accustomed to being that person you have created based on what you believe others want you to be and fail to acknowledge the authentic you. It is time to acknowledge your true feelings about what happened to you and deal with your true feeling about individuals who harmed you.

As you begin the healing process, being honest with yourself means understanding that you may have to tackle some hard thoughts and feelings about your childhood and the trauma you endured, but commit yourself to the process anyway. It is time to be honest, and admit that you are angry, disappointed, hurt, and maybe even suicidal.

Experiencing both positive and negative emotions is normal. Being honest about your feelings will provide you with a safe healing space. You may need time to assess your problems and be able to do so peacefully and without judgment or blame. Positive and negative emotions become problematic when they impact your life, work, health, and loved ones.

If you have experienced childhood trauma, you may have found yourself over the years searching for ways to distance yourself from the traumatic event by denying that the traumatic event has happened, disassociating yourself from the event, or repressing memories of what happened.

The dissociation that is a result of childhood trauma damages or even destroys your ability to be in touch with your true feelings, needs, and thoughts. You essentially learn to be what other people want you to be. You learned to internalize the pain all your life because "men are not supposed to cry," or "crying is a form of weakness." The stigma surrounding mental illness prevents you from getting the desperately needed help and support. If you internalize your pain, you will most likely be full of anger and resentment and struggling to maintain healthy relationships.

Childhood trauma can have a negative impact on your mental and physical health throughout your entire life. Sigmund Freud said that the first five years of a child's life shape the adult personality. A childhood marked with pain and trauma can affect your personality. You may have been a happy, fun child but have experienced emotional trauma, and you started to dissociate and become more isolated.

The trauma that you experience as a child can have an effect on your personality as an adult. Many mood and personality disorders are a result of early childhood abuse. It was also Freud who also said that people have the propensity to repeat patterns of behaviors that were traumatic in their earlier life.

As human beings, you seek comfort in what is familiar. This is often referred to as being a 'creature of habit.' This is why you can eat the same thing over and over again, or you attract the same kind of friends. There is nothing wrong with repetitive behaviors until those behaviors become harmful, like continually dating people who may emotionally and physically abuse you.

This is the time to revisit your past and be honest about the traumatic event that happened to you. The first step in your healing process is acknowledging that the event occurred. It is also imperative to acknowledge certain childhood experiences as trauma in the healing process. This will help you to understand how the trauma has affected you. Being honest about your experience and the effects of the trauma will help give meaning to your current problems and make sense of your struggles.

The second step is acknowledging that you are not responsible for what happened. It is important to recognize that what happened to you is real, and getting over it will take a process. You may have been told to Fake It Till You Make It (FITYMI). This phrase is about changing your behavior and trusting that your feelings will eventually change to match your behaviors.

It is based on the philosophy that what you think about the most is the thing that you manifest. It is not actually about being fake. It is about not allowing your feelings to influence your actions but rather making your actions influence your thoughts. For instance, you may not feel like engaging in social activities but engage anyway. You may not feel like moving forward but move forward anyway.

It is also common teaching among the religious community with the revised aphorism of 'faith it until you make it.' The idea of this aphorism is to display what you want until it comes into existence. The bible tells us in Mark 11:23, "For verily I say unto you, That whosoever shall say unto the mountain, Be thou removed, and be cast into the sea; and shall not doubt in his heart, but shall believe that those thing which he saith shall come to pass; he shall have whatsoever he saith." If you "say" it and "not doubt" it but "believe" it, then you "shall have" it.

The bible does not give a timeframe between when you say it and when you receive it. However, what is said is that you must display faith and wait until it comes to past. You act as if you have what you have already prayed for before you actually receive it.

A negative consequence of FITYMI is that living in a constant state of inauthenticity will negatively affect your mental state in the long term. You can only fake it for so long without becoming an inauthentic version of yourself. At this point, you become more interested in changing how others see you rather than actually healing, which is the point of FITYMI.

You were and still are not responsible for what happened to you. You were not able to control what happened to you. The 'adult you' had no way to protect the 'child you'. You did not let yourself down. You lacked the power to respond to the traumatic events that happened to you. You could not protect yourself or leave the situation. You were a child. You did not choose your trauma; your trauma happened to you. You may have blamed yourself for things that were completely out of your control. The childhood trauma you experienced has left a wound like all other wounds, and it will take time to heal.

The effects of childhood trauma can continue into your adult life because no matter how hard you have tried to move on from the trauma, there is still a traumatized child living inside you, a child crying to get free and a child crying out to be loved and valued. All children want to be loved, especially by their parents, and if you do not receive that love, you begin to think it is because of you. In turn, you try to become the child you believe your parents or caregiver could love. Even then, it was not enough.
This lack of love made you feel hopeless and unlovable. Because you were neglected, rejected, or abused, the sense of being unloved and unlovable carried over into adulthood and affected all areas of your life. You created an inauthentic version of yourself to present to people around you.

By doing this, you lost the person you were created to become. Now you live terrified that if you change to your God-created version of self, people will no longer love or accept you. You are now living with the past trauma but forced to live a false narrative you created. You hide your feelings and the truth about your trauma. Many of you have become highly inauthentic people who are overly worried about others' opinions of you.

Childhood trauma may have impacted you to the point that you have become a different person. When people tell you just to be yourself, do you know who that person is? Do you know who that person would be if you had not experienced that traumatic event? I was talking with a friend, and she said she had been lost in her pain for so long that she did not know who she really should be.

She was tired of being everything for everybody. She sat down with tears flowing from her eyes like a river and cried out to God to reveal the person He created her to be on this earth. The person that He spoke about in Jeremiah 1:5, where he said, "Before I formed thee in the belly, I knew thee; and before thou camest forth out of the womb I sanctified thee, and I ordained thee a prophet unto the nations." He answered her prayer.

You may want to cry out to the Lord for your authentic version of yourself to be revealed to you. If you do not have a sense of self, you will always change to avoid abandonment to ensure everyone likes you. A person who has experienced a childhood trauma sometimes becomes a people pleaser. People- pleasing is a way of coping with a lack of security in a relationship.

You may find it difficult to talk about your childhood trauma and its effect on your mental wellness. You are not alone. Most people are uncomfortable talking about the hard things, choosing to ignore them, cover them up, and even turn away those who may know and could bring them up. You must find a safe place to openly and honestly discuss how you feel.

Digging up your past that you have hidden since childhood will not be easy initially. The culture of shame that has been created may make it difficult to speak about it. There is a broken child inside every adult with unresolved trauma waiting to be free. This is why an seventy-year-old can recall events and still feel the same pain she experienced in her childhood.

CHAPTER 3

RECLAIM YOUR POWER

*H*ow do you move forward after a traumatic, life-changing event happens in your life? The most important thing is not to get stuck in your pain. Healing from trauma is a difficult process. It does not happen overnight. It is very common for someone who has experienced a traumatic childhood to develop feelings of helplessness. Feelings of helplessness can make you feel and act like a victim, causing you to make choices based on your past pain.

An essential step in reclaiming your power is forgiveness. Forgiveness is the initial step, but not the only one, in taking away the person's power over your life. Forgiveness is a process of choosing to let go of the negative emotions related to the trauma regardless of whether the person deserves it or not.

You may never get the apology you have been waiting for all your life. The person who harmed you may already be deceased or unwilling to communicate with you. You may not be willing to forgive the person because you are waiting for that person to return and say they are sorry.

You have been trained from childhood that forgiveness requires an apology. Remember being forced to tell someone you were sorry even if you did not mean it. You had well-meaning parents, but this forced apology conditioned you that you required an apology to forgive the person and move on from the hurt.

When you were a child, do you remember saying, "I'm not your friend anymore because you hurt my feelings and did not apologize?" Well, maybe the person was not truly apologetic, but you felt better because at least they apologized, even if they were not sincere. People would do the same thing over and over to you because they were not sincerely apologetic, but they learned that they did not have to mean it; they just had to say it.

If you are constantly apologizing for something you did not mean to do, let me encourage you to change your behavior. Over-apologizing is sometimes rooted in childhood trauma where you were forced to apologize to avoid conflict or harm to yourself. It is a trauma response from having experienced a difficult and traumatic childhood.

Sometimes those who harmed you will ask for forgiveness, but most of the time you will not get that long-awaited apology. They may genuinely feel bad for how they treated you, but they may never return for many different reasons. Some people will not apologize because they do not want to admit they were wrong or that the abuse happened.

Look at forgiveness as a step toward becoming free from your past. Forgiveness allows you to release yourself from the grips of the offense. Forgiveness is also an opportunity not to allow the pain to define you. Forgiveness does not mean you are okay with the trauma the individual caused; it means you are freeing yourself from the pain of it.

You may have heard people say this somewhat misleading statement that you should *forgive and forget*. It is unrealistic to think that if you have experienced childhood trauma, you will or even should forget what happened to you. Research has shown that people with trauma can suppress a memory or force it out of their awareness but not forget it.

You may have also heard someone say, "I'll forgive you, but I will never forget what you have done." You may have even said this yourself. It appears to suggest that forgetting what happened is necessary to forgive the person. It is not! The bible only instructs us to forgive one another (Matthew 6:14).

There may be many reasons why you do not want to forgive the person. You may not want to forgive because you feel that not forgiving is payback to your offender as if you are punishing the person who harmed you. I have heard so many people say that I will never forgive someone for what they did to me.

Refusing to forgive keeps you emotionally attached to the trauma and the person who harmed you. Studies have shown that living with unforgiveness affects not only your spiritual health but also your physical health. Unforgiveness causes bitterness in your heart. The bitterness often leads to anger. In Ephesians 4:31, the bible tells us to "Let all bitterness, and wrath, and anger, and clamour, and evil speaking, be put away from you, with all malice". As you forgive, you will begin to see a shift in the narrative you created around the trauma.

Changing the person's action or self is not the purpose of forgiveness. Forgiveness is not a human response but rather a divine one. It is a matter of the heart. It begins in the heart. The bible states in Matthew 6:24 states, "No man can serve two masters: for either he will hate the one, and love the other; or else he will hold to the one, and despise the other. Ye cannot serve God and mammon."

Also, in 1 John 4:20, the bible states, "If a man say, I love God, and hateth his brother, he is a liar; for he that loveth not his brother whom he hath seen, how can he love God whom he hath not seen?" You cannot commit yourself to the works of God yet, walk contrary to his word. The bible can be summarized in one word, love—the love for God and the love for man. According to the bible, love is forgiveness.

However, no one should force you to forgive the person. You should move to forgive in your own time. Forcing you to forgive will take your power in the same way as the person who initially harmed you. Forgiving is a choice. Chose to forgive in your own time.

Making sense of past traumatic events in your life may not be easy. Healing may seem impossible. Just because the experience is over does not mean you have not been deeply affected. For far too many years, you have been defined by what happened to you.

When you allow rage and unforgiveness to destroy your joy, your purpose, and who you are, you hand over victory to the person who has wronged you. Chances are they have moved on with their lives without any thoughts of you, oblivious or uncaring to the wrong they have done to you.

What should you do now? You take steps towards healing. You take back your power when you choose to work on healing and learning how to truly enjoy your life. Whoever caused you pain does not win.

You can now go on to have an emotionally healthy life, overcome the tragedies of your past, and find joy again. The good news is that you can still heal even if you refuse to forgive the person who harmed you. Through healing, forgiving will eventually come.

Forgiveness exercise:

1. Write a letter about your feelings about the traumatic experience to the person who offended you. Do this with the intention of destroying it. Read the letter aloud as if you are talking directly to the person who harmed you. Then, destroy the letter as an act of moving on from your past.

2. Write another letter of forgiveness to the person who harmed you. Read the letter aloud as if you are talking to God about your forgiveness toward that person. When you feel that you are ready, pray for that person. Keep the letter. Periodically revisit the letter and read it aloud until you feel ready to pray for the individual.

3. Write the names of every person that you have offended. How many people would you have to ask for forgiveness. Should they forgive you?

CHAPTER 4

EXPERIENCE YOUR EMOTIONS

The worse thing that has happened to you is the worst thing that has happened to you. The trauma that happened to you does not have to define you; it will not if you do not allow it, but you have to fight with everything that is in you not to allow this to happen. Most of the time, it does not come easy. You may feel many emotions, from fear, anxiety, numbness, or detachment. It is normal to have strong emotions following a traumatic event.

When it comes to your emotions, you may tend to repress them, deny them, or tell them to go away. If you have been told, as I have, that thinking about negative things will bring negative experiences into your lives, you may have learned to hide your emotions. Yet, those negative thoughts keep playing in your head like a broken record.

If you are playing a harmful event repeatedly in your head, it is also playing in your heart. Proverbs 4:23 tell us, "Keep thy heart with all diligence; for out of it arc the issues of life." The verse says that whatever comes out of your heart manifest in your life. Possible evidence that your repetitive thoughts are problematic is if someone says you are complaining too much or it becomes a problem in your relationships.

When you experience unresolved trauma, it is transmitted and stored in your body. It can manifest in many ways, causing physical, emotional, and mental distress in the body. You may feel trapped in your emotions and unable to escape from the memory of the traumatic experience and the painful feelings of the experience.

It has been said that your brain responds the same to both emotional pain and physical pain. This means there is no difference in how the brain processes pain. Studies have shown that chronic pain might be caused by physical injury and stress, and emotional issues.

Social and cultural taboos about men crying may tell them they are not supposed to cry. They grow up seeing crying as a form of weakness, leading to internalized shame about tears. If you internalize your pain, it may result in you being an angry and often unhealthy person. Those emotions have to go somewhere. If you do not experience your emotions, you will become them.

Sit with your emotions and let your feelings flow. Do not be ashamed or afraid to acknowledge your feelings. Let your body respond the way it wants or needs to respond. If you want to yell, yell. If you want to cry, cry. You have been taught to hold your emotions for far too long.

Emotions Exercise

1. Write down as many positive childhood experiences that you can remember. Meditate on these memories for the next seven days and write your feelings in your journal.

2. What did you notice about your feelings in those seven days? Were you able to express your feelings easier as the days went by? What did you notice about your emotions?

CHAPTER 5

ASK FOR HELP

After abuse has ended, the journey to your healing may be a long process. You have been through a traumatic experience that could potentially impact the rest of your life. Are you like so many other people who do not ask for help to deal with their mental health struggles?

There may be many barriers to why you do not ask for help. Fear and shame are common reasons that prevent people from asking for help. Maybe you have been told, like so many others, to "stop blaming others for your problems," and you are hesitant about coming forward and admitting that you need help.

Many of you may not want to talk about their mental health for the fear that they will get discriminated against if someone finds out you are in mental health treatment. No one wants to be labeled as *mentally ill* or *crazy*. You do not want people to think that you do not have it altogether since this is the false narrative that you have created about yourself.

Trauma can rewire the brain and disrupt healthy brain information flow. When the brain goes into stress or is stuck in stress, it leads to physical changes and a complicated ripple of life-altering symptoms. As a survivor of childhood trauma, you must rewire your brains to experience healing and recovery.

The hardest and most courageous step in the healing process is to ask for help. I think back to my little 13-year-old friend Addie from earlier in the book. Addie was asking for help, but her grandmother did not see a need to get her help. I did not talk to Addie's grandmother, so I do not know why she did not want her granddaughter to attend therapy. It could be a financial reason, or she sincerely thought Addie no longer needed therapy.

I only know that you, the person seeking treatment, are more aware of your mental health needs than anyone else. No one should tell you not to seek help from a mental health practitioner if you believe you need it. Your decision to seek help should be based on your needs rather than their personal thoughts. Addie is too young to decide on her health, but you are not. Healing from a traumatic childhood will require you to actively seek help from a mental health practitioner.

Asking for help is difficult for someone who has experienced trauma as a child. The biggest reason that you will not ask for or accept help may be because you still feel a sense of betrayal. You do not know who you can trust when your trust is violated at a young age.

Unfortunately, some resist talking with a counselor about their troubles because of the stigma attached to consulting a mental health counselor, especially in the African American and minority communities. As a minority, you may also hold stigmatizing beliefs regarding mental health treatment. You may have been taught that going to a mental health therapist is taboo, and you do not believe that talking to an outsider about your problems is appropriate. Believing the stigma leads to you not being truthful about your mental health and getting the care you need.

As Christians, you are expected to be strong and resilient, and you should depend totally on God. You are taught to just pray about it. Prayer is vitally important for healing to happen. Luke 18:1 says, "… men ought always to pray, and not to faint."

The problem, however, comes when you attempt to live up to the faulty cultural paradigm of being spiritually weak if you ask for mental health help. Research has shown that African Americans are less likely than other ethnic groups to seek mental health treatment. All healing will not happen in the church healing line. Some healing will take place in a therapeutic environment. A person with a physical illness will go to church for prayer, but they will also go to their physician. You can also do both.

There are trained and certified specialists and experts who can help you work through your trauma. Do not be afraid to talk with someone. If you feel ready to discuss the traumatic event that happened to you, contact a therapist to talk about your experiences and your feelings.

CHAPTER 6

TELL YOUR STORY

*Y*ou have a story to tell, and it matters. Your story may be the catalyst to help others who have gone through trauma navigate the healing process. Your voice has been silenced for too long; you deserve to be heard.

You may be unaware of how trauma has affected your life; you just know that you are hurting. Many of you who have gone through trauma have not told your story. Either you are afraid to share your story for fear of being judged, you believe that no one wants to hear your story, you are ashamed, you are still protecting the person who harmed you, or there is a shift in belief that you have created about yourself. For instance, you may believe that because the trauma happened to you, you are weak for not protecting yourself, or your story is so devastating that you do not want to relive it. These are just some reasons for not wanting to tell your story. However, one of the major steps in the healing process is letting out the pain. You can do this by telling your story.

Continue sharing your story with people that you trust. By talking about your story about the trauma, you can be on the road to renewed trust and recovery. Naturally, many of you who have experienced childhood trauma do your best to avoid these painful memories of the trauma that you experienced because, honestly, who would willingly expose themselves to even more pain?

Unfortunately, avoiding trauma can sometimes be more harmful than helpful. Avoidance may result in the trauma becoming more painful. You can tell your story through a powerful technique called trauma narrative. It allows you to confront and overcome your painful childhood trauma memories through storytelling. It allows you to make sense of your trauma experience by repeatedly telling your story through verbal, written, or artistic means. There are many techniques, but any technique should be with a trained psychotherapist or mental health practitioner.

You can find a trusted friend or family member and tell them your trauma story. When you decide to tell your story, it is up to you to create boundaries to telling your story. You decide how much you want to share and to what audience you want to share your story. For most people, knowing the details of the trauma is not as important as you telling it. Your healing does not depend on how much information you give people. Telling your story is about releasing the pains of your past and the control it has over your life.

Do not tell your story to just anyone. Everyone is not capable of hearing your story. Be careful in sharing your story with someone who does not have the emotional capacity to handle your story. They may have unresolved trauma, and your story may trigger their trauma responses. When it comes to sharing your story in a personal relationship, consider their character and the ability of the person to hold your story. Confide in someone who will respect your story and keep it private until you are ready to share it publicly.

Finally, talk to a therapist. There is something therapeutic in telling your story. Telling the story to a licensed professional can help you process the experience and navigate through your feelings relating to the trauma. When you experience deep pain, it comes out in your voice. The person at your job who everyone calls mean and hateful may be a person with deep-seated hurt or unresolved trauma. Through retelling your story, you will find the distress and shame relating to it will subside.

Tell you story exercise:

1. Practice telling your story in a mirror. You are responsible for setting the boundaries for telling your story. Identify what information you are ready to share. The more you tell your story cannot change the past, but it can help you shift how the memories affect you in the present.

CHAPTER 7

HEALTHY "ME" TIME

And the apostles gathered themselves together unto Jesus, and told him all things, both what they had done, and what they had taught. And he said unto them, Come ye yourselves apart into a desert place, and rest a while: for there were many coming and going, and they had no leisure so much as to eat. And they departed into a desert place by ship privately.

—Mark 6:30-32

And on the seventh day, God finished his work that he had done, and he rested on the seventh day from all his work which he had done.

—Genesis 2:2

*T*aking time for yourself is essential to your healing. Taking "me" time is a means of self-care. Self-care is about taking time to rest and giving your body the necessary downtime to rejuvenate itself. The first thing that you have to reconcile with is that taking "me" time is not being selfish. Taking "Me" time is not about being lazy. Nowadays, when someone say they need some "Me" time, people apply a negative connotation to the meaning of "me" time.

Your relationship with God is the most important in your life. The relationship that you have with yourself is the next important one. You cannot love others without first loving yourself. It can be challenging to rebuild your life after a traumatic event.

I remember trying to put a puzzle together that had some pieces missing. The missing pieces made putting the puzzle together a little more challenging. Regardless, I was successful in putting the puzzle together. As I stood there looking at the 1,000-piece puzzle with the pieces missing, it reminded me of life. Each missing piece of the puzzle represents different problems that we each encountered in our life.

Trauma is one of the missing puzzle pieces. You can live without it, but it is difficult to live with it. When you experience a traumatic event, a ripple effect happens. Living with the effects of trauma impacts your mental and physical health.

Some of the problems you may encounter are the inability to rest properly and chronic fatigue. Setting aside time to rejuvenate your body, mind, and spirit is important. If you find yourself acting out of character over some of the smallest situations and with certain people, you may need some "me" time.

Give yourself permission to take care of yourself. There is no special way to make time for yourself, and you do not have to follow a certain protocol. The important thing is to take time away to focus on yourself. Remember, you are in control and can make any decision concerning your life. It is all about you! There are many things that you can do for self-care. Self-care is unique to the person's life and needs. You can do anthing you like to do such as:

- Visit a friend
- Exercise

- Watch television
- Meditate
- Go out for coffee
- Sleep in
- Read
- Go to church (religious event)

Self-care is about more than finding ways to hang out. It plays a role in both your mental and physical health. It is about taking time to care for yourself mentally, physically, emotionally, and spiritually. It is necessary for improving your health and living a stress-free life. Take control of your life. Embrace your healing, love yourself, and rest.

CHAPTER 8

ENVISION YOUR HEALING!

*H*ealing from your childhood trauma is hard, but it is possible. Envision yourself healed. How often have you heard someone say, "If it is God's will then I will have this or that?" Let me share some revelation with you. If it is in his word, it is in his will. The bible tells us in Mark 5:34, "And he said unto her, Daughter, thy faith hath made thee whole...."

What is faith? Hebrews 11:1 states, "Now faith is the substance of things hoped for, the evidence of things not seen." Faith is not seen (natural); faith is believed (divine). You must see what you want before you get what you want. Once you understand childhood trauma and what it looks like in the present moment, it is time to accept it for what it is and the impact it has on your life.

It is now time for you to let go of your past trauma and begin to write your future based on your newfound freedom. This may seem difficult in the beginning. You must give yourself permission to be free. Take time to write the traumatized child in you a letter to release him or her to be free from the past pain of abuse and to live. Notice that I did not say to "live again" because some of you have not lived since you experienced your trauma.

So many of you who experience childhood trauma become trapped in your abusive past. You are living in a constant state of hyperarousal and preparing yourself for the next attack or life-altering event. Hyperarousal refers to an abnormal state of anxiety that happens when you think about a traumatic event. Your body will still respond to the threat as if the threat is still present.

Sadly, some of you believe that you are worthless, unlovable, and fear being close to others. These are all normal responses to an abusive situation. However, to live stuck in these lies essentially gives the one who traumatized you the power.

You cannot change what happened to you; it was not your fault. You do have control over what you do now. For far too many years, you have been defined by what happened to you. You then became known for what you became. For example, you may have become angry and become known as being 'difficult' or 'mean.'

The following are steps to changing the narrative that you have created about yourself based on what happened to your healing:

Challenge Your Negative Self-Talk

A negative self-talk is defined as a critical thought about yourself. Your negative thoughts may be a product of your upbringing, conditioning, or both. While everyone experiences negative thinking every now and then, negative thinking becomes problematic when you continually think negatively about yourself and the world around you until it interferes with your normal everyday functioning.

Are you constantly questioning whether you are good enough, capable enough, or talented enough, or if you tend to focus more on what you did wrong than what you did right, the ten percent that you did wrong matters more than the ninety percent that you did right then it is an indication that your negative thoughts should be challenged?

Negative thoughts are also attributed to problems such as social anxiety, depression, stress, and low self-esteem. The key to changing your negative thoughts is to identify the negative thoughts and replace them with positive ones. How do you know if a thought is negative and should be challenged? Start by asking yourself these four questions:

1. Is it what the word of God says about you?
2. Would you allow a friend or someone that you love to say the same thing about themselves?
3. Would you feel comfortable if someone close to you heard you say it?
4. Would you say these things to your friend or loved one?

If you answer "no" to any of these questions, this indicates the presence of negative self-talk.

Self-talk is your inner voice in your head that sometimes encourages you but frequently degrades, judges, and self-sabotages you. Self-talk can be beneficial when it is positive. It can be harmful if it is negative, saying such things as, "I cannot do anything right" or "I am such an idiot."

The key to challenging your negative self-talk or voice in your head is to become aware of when you have negative self-talk and when it talks to you, talk back to it. When it tells you that you are not good enough, tell it that it is a lie and replace any negative thoughts with positive words that God says about you. If your inner voice says that you are fat, speak back to it, I AM fearfully and wonderfully made, and marvelous are the works of God.

I like to begin my affirmations with I AM following the teaching of God. God used the words I AM to reveal to Moses the promises found in His name. Just as the rainbow reminds us of His promise not to destroy the earth with water again, using I AM reminds you of His promise to be whatever you need Him to be in your life.

However, you should make your affirmations personal to you and your situation.

Challenging Negative Self-Talk Exercise

1. An quick and easy exercise to help you challenge your negative self-talk is that every time you say something negative about yourself, write it down.

2. Review how many instances you have written down at the end of the week.

3. Replace your negative self-talk with positive words and recite these as affirmations to yourself while standing in your mirror.

This exercise will make you keenly aware of how many conversations you have with your inner voice and what your inner voice is telling you about yourself. If you want to change your negative perception of yourself, you have to change what you are saying to yourself. When negative self-talk begins, shift your thinking to the positive in your life. This is the most powerful way to change the negative self-talk.

Make Necessary Life Changes

As you begin the healing process, caring for yourself should become more of a priority. Mental health treatment can help you heal from trauma, but there's more to the recovery process. Lifestyle changes should follow up treatment.

A lifestyle change may mean removing some toxic people from your life. The truth is some people in your present should be in your past. They are toxic and negatively affect your life and mental health. If you keep them in your life, your future will die because you are holding on to your past.

Sometimes you hold on to people whom you know are not good for you because:

1. You are afraid of being alone.
2. You stay with what is familiar.
3. You are afraid of change.

You may want to change your diet to lose the weight you want to lose so you can become a healthier and happier version of yourself. Get that gym membership that you have been contemplating getting. Make at least one lifestyle change in your daily life that will promote personal growth and empowering experience.

Mindfulness Meditation

Mindfulness has become a much-talked-about practice for a very good reason because it has so many benefits. First of all, it is easy to get started with mindfulness, and the cost is minimal. You do not need any special tools, just yourself, a quiet space, and the most important thing that you will need is time. You already have the capacity to be present, and meditating does not require you to change a thing about who you are.

Mindfulness is the basic human ability to be fully present, aware of where you are and what you are doing, and not overly reactive or overwhelmed by what is happening around you. Mindfulness describes a practice of focused attention and awareness.

As many of you probably have been, I was taught that if you are a Christian, you should not meditate. This belief most likely came from their misunderstanding of the meaning of the word meditate. Meditate, in its simplest term, means "focus." It comes from the Latin word 'to ponder.'

It is easy to understand why many Christians, especially older Christians, shy away from the act or practice of meditation because, in the past, meditation has been associated with religious traditions, particularly Buddhism. It does not help that when Hollywood portrays meditation, it is usually with Buddhist Monks sitting with their legs crossed, eyes closed, and chanting.

Meditation is not a sin, as some Christians also think. You are not praying to a foreign god. Meditation can include speaking the scriptures, praying the scriptures, or thinking about the scriptures. The bible speaks about meditating on the word of God and the reward for doing so.

> *This Book of the Law shall not depart from your mouth, but you shall meditate in it day and night, that you may observe to do according to all that is written in it. For then you will make your way prosperous, and then you will have good success.*
>
> *—Joshua 1:8*

> *Blessed is the man that walketh not in the counsel of the ungodly, nor standeth in the way of sinners, nor sitteth in the seat of the scornful. But his delight is in the law of the Lord; and in his law doth he meditates day and night.*
>
> *—Psalm 1:1-3*

Research has shown that meditation can have both physiological and psychological benefits. The bible promises us prosperity and success. Some of the benefits of meditating on God's word include:

- Reduces stress
- Controls anxiety
- Promotes emotional health and well being
- Improves focus
- Prospers you and makes you successful!

Mindfulness Meditation Exercise

Find at least 3-5 biblical scriptures relating to your situation, read God's written words, meditate on them, speak them aloud, and pray according to the spirit over the scriptures. Do this every day for the next 30 days. Listen to your thoughts. Write down anything specific that you hear.

Journaling

Thus speaketh the Lord God of Israel, saying, Write thee all the words that I have spoken unto thee in a book

—Jeremiah 30:2

Research has shown that journaling can have a powerful impact on your psyche. It is a tool most often used as part of the mindfulness practice. It can be an alternative to or a part of your mindfulness meditation. It is a way of documenting what you may have heard during your quiet time with the Lord.

Journaling is a form of record-keeping for your thoughts, feelings, insights, and more. The great thing about journaling is there is no right or wrong way to do it. It does not have to look the same from day to day. It could be your thoughts and feelings one day; the next day, you may write about your goals and ambitions. The important thing is to be consistent.

Your entries can be written, drawn, or typed. It can be on paper or your computer. An alternative to writing in your journal is to doodle (scribble or draw) in your journal. Do not worry about proper grammar or spelling. You are the only one who will see your journal unless you share it.

Research has shown that doodling can help mitigate the negative effects of stress. All you need to get started is a piece of paper and a drawing tool. It has been proven that the rhythmic and repetitive motion of your drawing will reduce your stress and anxiety. There is no need to look at Pinterest or YouTube for ideas on how to get started; just start. Your focus should not be on how good your doodling looks; the overall goal is for you to control your thoughts and not allow your thoughts to control you. Surprisingly, you will get better with time.

When you initially start writing in your journal, it may seem daunting. I encourage you to continue. The key to success is to create a writing routine and schedule a time to journal to help you stay on track. Set realistic expectations. If you know that you are not an early riser, do not set your journaling time for five o'clock in the mornings. This will only set you up for failure, and you will get discouraged when you do not wake up to journal.

Some of the benefits of journaling include:

- Reduces stress and anxiety
- Provides a mean to process emotions
- Better sleep

Journaling Exercise

1. Start your mornings with 10 - 15 minutes of uninterrupted journaling time. If you are not a morning person, set aside 10-15 minutes every night. Be consistent. You will find that the more you journal, the longer the time you will spend journaling.

2. There is no specific way to journal. A suggestion would be to write at the top of your journal page, write "I'm Grateful for…" List three items that you are grateful for and expound on what you've written. This will get you started.

Trust Yourself Again

"Have the courage to follow your heart and intuition. They somehow already know what you truly want to become."

—Steve Jobs

How are you supposed to trust again when trust has been broken? Trusting people again may take a long time after your trust has been violated, but it is possible. Trusting yourself is the most difficult part. You have to first trust yourself to be able to care for yourself.

The first step is to accept that you did not fail yourself. The next step is to change the way that you talk to yourself. Affirmations are positive statements that can help you to challenge and overcome self-sabotaging and negative thoughts. They are another way to help you to make the changes in your life necessary for healing. Writing affirmations down and saying them aloud is another way to heal from childhood trauma.

Our thoughts create our experiences. You are affirming and creating your life experiences with every word and every thought. If you are thinking negative thoughts, you are creating negative experiences. Affirmations help to retrain your thinking. Affirmations are statements that are repeated to help challenge negative thoughts and encourage positive changes in your life. Using affirmations to change your thought pattern requires regular practice. Christian affirmations are more than just repeating words.

Christian affirmations are about confirming what the word of God says about you. Words are powerful! You do not need science to tell you there is power in your words. The bible tells us in Proverbs 18:21 that "Death and life are in the power of the tongue."

God has given you words to either bless you or curse you. According to the scriptures, you should watch carefully over your words. One way that Jesus was revealed is as the *Word* made flesh. There is power in the spoken word. Afterall, God *spoke* the world into existence.

> *Casting down imaginations, and every high thing that exalteth itself against the knowledge of God, and bringing into captivity every thought to the obedience of Christ.*
>
> **—2 Corinthians 10:5**

Finally, brethren, whatsoever things are true, whatsoever things are honest, whatsoever things are just, whatsoever things are pure, whatsoever things are lovely, whatsoever things are of good report; if there be any virtue, and if there be any praise, think on these things.

—Philippians 4:8

Let Go of Your Fears

For God hath not given us the spirit of fear, but of power, and of love, and of a sound mind.

—2 Timothy 2:7

I sought the LORD, and he heard me, And delivered me from all my fears.

—Psalm 34:4-6

The first scripture tells you that God did not give you the spirit of fear, while the second scripture lets you know that if you have fear, God can deliver you from it.

Fear is a hard-wired emotion in the brain. It is an alert system that notifies us of danger to keep us safe. Fear is an emotion that can protect as well as paralyze you. Fear robs you of enjoying your life. One of my cousins had a debilitating fear of riding on the highway. As a result, she had to depend on certain relatives to drive her places. She could not live her life to the fullest because her constraints bound her.

Feeling safe and learning to trust again after experiencing trauma can be very difficult, particularly for repeated or long-term physical, sexual, or emotional abuse. It may seem elusive, but it is not. Trauma activates the "fight or flight" response in the brain. Severe trauma can cause your brain to stay in that mode or quickly return to that place of fear when your brain recognizes a similar act and is triggered.

How do you get rid of your fears? The bible tells us in Matthew 17:21, "Howbeit this kind goeth not out but by prayer and fasting." The benefits of spiritual fasting are seen throughout the bible. One of the most popular scriptures on fasting is in the book of Esther, where Esther fasted to have divine favor. Prayer and fasting are both biblical ways of hearing and receiving from God.

CONCLUSION

No One Was There For Me is a heart-breaking phrase that I often hear when speaking to people who have experienced trauma. It was also a statement that I heard the late Naomi Judd say during a television interview about her battle with mental illness.

Memories of the abuse and the pain associated with your childhood trauma often carry over into adulthood. The unresolved trauma and pains from your childhood are stored in the operating system of your mind called the subconscious.

As you may recall from what I discussed earlier in the book, your inner child is part of your subconscious. Your inner child holds your unresolved trauma and all its pain. It carries both the negative and positive beliefs formed in childhood.

The manifestations of trauma symptoms are complex and unique to the person who experienced the trauma. There is no one-size-fits-all of what trauma and healing should look like from one person to the next. Trauma is indiscriminate, meaning it affects people from all cultures and backgrounds.

You can be high functioning yet suffer from the effects of trauma. The misconception is that because you are successful, it means that you are not affected by your traumatic childhood. They do not know that your fears, trauma, and hurt run far deeper than the natural eye can see and lingers in both the brain and body.

Many of you are still hesitant about disclosing your trauma, choosing to take the trauma to your graves instead. As a reminder, unresolved trauma can result in you having broken relationships, addictions, diseases, and, as mentioned earlier, even a shorter life expectancy.

I want you to know that help is available for you. You are not alone. There is light at the end of the tunnel and a better life on the other side of your healing. This book can help your inner child heal and thrive, allowing you to become the authentic person whom God created you to be. Yes, your soul is wounded but ask the Lord to restore your soul as David did in Psalm 23.

If you want to heal from the trauma, you must begin by facing it — bravely, and one BREATHE at a time.